Love Through a Lens

Mattie A. Scott

Mattie A. Scott

Copyright © 2015 Mattie A. Scott

All rights reserved.

ISBN-10: 0692549722
ISBN-13: 978-0692549728

DARRYL,

We were only meant to be together for a season.

I understand that now.

Thank you, for the good & bad times,

the ups & the downs

Each lesson I learned I will hold dear and take it with me.

Through our love, I have been inspired

broken down and pieced back together.

I have grown.

I have known love in its purest form.

I have acquired the most precious gift

any man could have ever given me.

Thank you for being by my side

when I needed you the most

but allowing me room to deal with issues

that affected me the most.

Thank you for spoiling me with patience

and giving me room to grow

into who I needed to be

without you.

I love you.

Love Through a Lens

Mattie A. Scott

ACKNOWLEDGMENTS

Thank you to those who made these words possible.

Without knowing you, I would have fewer words to write.

I would have no inspiration to draw upon.

I would have no love to gaze upon.

I would have no knowledge of other worlds.

Mattie A. Scott

I closed my eyes as his breath softly covered my senses. I couldn't resist the smoothness of his skin as he curled his body next to mine, invading my space.

I cared not about the time of day or who was begging for my attention. All I knew was this man and his skin were pleasing to me.

I had an appetite, but for what I did not know.

This was unfamiliar territory to me. His fingers found their way into my hair and gently tugged away at my ponytail. Resting his head in my hair, he closed his eyes and drifted off to sleep.

*****

Sometimes I stare at him.

My eyes gloss over at the thought of him staring back.

His gentle voice rings through my ears, snapping my attention back to reality.

A shiver runs up my spine as he comes closer to me, my heart aching for his acceptance.

Slowly I close my eyes, anticipating his embrace.

*****

There is rarely a day that goes by where I don't think of him.

His calm demeanor graces my thoughts and I long to be as he is.

He was a gentleman, filling me with words of wisdom and kindness I knew not before him.

I only knew what he told me and to me it was good.

He could do no wrong.

*****

I wait patiently for him to come to me.

I don't know where he comes from but that does not matter.

He says I am his final destination.

The ride is a thrill only I can give to him...or so he says.

He has a way with words.

*****

My flesh has grown older and wiser.

Sensitive to touch and gentle to feel.

I long for the moment he will hold me.

Tell me how much he enjoys my body.

His admiration is what I crave most.

Giving delight to his senses.

*****

He blew me away.

His scent clouded my senses as he drifted by me.

His figure draped with a plain white shirt and black basketball shorts that hung slightly low.

He stared at me, as if he were taking me into his soul.

I felt a lump swell in my throat as I panicked.

Nervous laughter escaped and I felt foolish.

I was in love.

*****

I feel the tide rising with the evening moon.

The light is bright and heavy, beaming down on me.

His image races across my mind as I close my eyes and breathe in the ocean air.

The cologne of the sea.

Cold water across my feet, gritty sand in my teeth.

I lay down, my hair now covered in salt and sand.

Cold water creeps down my throat and my eyes sting.

All I smell is the ocean.

All I feel is moonlight.

*****

I consumed him.

I gave him everything I had inside.

The pains of my soul poured out onto the bed.

I heard him call my name and it burned my ears.

He reached out for me, grasping for his life, but I had consumed him in his entirety.

I traced my fingers against his forehead and kissed his lips.

I stood up and watched him sleep.

The stickiness of my love covered him.

*****

His love makes my chest burn.

I feel the contents of my stomach creep up my throat, gagging me till I can no longer control it.

My knees ache, my legs feel like thin rubber.

I have lost all control over my body.

I feel weak and helpless.

I felt myself falling to the ground, hands gripping my own head as I hit the bottom of my soul.

*****

I prayed he would return to me.

His voice echoed in my soul and I missed him.

Truly I did.

His skin was smooth and my soul ached when he wasn't around.

The morning sun burned my chest as I looked out the window, hoping to see his figure.

I felt nothing and everything equally.

I wasn't whole without him and his love I would die for...I would die for...

*****

I laid down next to nothing and felt my face burn with salty tears.

Next to nothing hurt worse than nothing at all.

At times I would rather not know the feeling of love than to be hurting so deeply for what I have lost.

His soul no longer yearns for me, I am no longer loved.

I have lost the war.

*****

Through him I learn about life, love and myself.

My foolish thoughts bubble out my mouth and foam with desire.

I crave his mind, the very essence of what makes him unique.

In his own ways he possess the power to influence me.

I hope that he tells me every thought he has ever had and every lie to hold me back.

He is the world as I have ever known it.

*****

I lowered myself onto the floor and closed my eyes.

The thought of him holding her burned my lids and I called out to every god I ever abandoned.

I cried for help.

I cried for me.

I cried for her.

For she will fall into the same trap I am in.

She will hate herself in order to love him.

His love is like gravity.

Constantly pulling you in until you orbit with nothing left.

Her soul will be lost.

She will become one of his many moons.

****

For a minute I didn't know where I was or where I was going.

And it felt good.

To be completely unaware of my surroundings.

To be away from him in my own silence.

I felt alive and well.

And all was good.

I felt nothing more than what I was born with and life was still full of meaning.

I just haven't found it yet.

*****

When he left me I was scared.

I knew I had nothing left and nothing left to give.

I didn't know anything other than that man.

He fed and nursed me and gave life to my soul.

I was sure he was a god of many lands.

And for him I scraped my knees when I gave him my praise.

*****

Every fragment I had left over from our love was lunged deep in my skin.

I felt each piece, knowing this was all I had left of him.

He was done with me.

I was useless at this point and I had nothing to hold me together but myself, which was a crumbling mess.

When did I become so weak that I needed to depend on him?

*****

He came back to me last night.

He said he had been traveling.

I asked where he went and if he learned anything.

His reply was simple:

There is a lesson in absence.

There are too many people in the world to settle

Until you realize the one thing you have the most desire for is missing and you can't bear to settle for less.

*****

His breath graced the back of my neck and he bent down to my level.

His eyes locked with mine and I felt fear creep under my lashes.

My heart felt like it had leaped from my chest and onto the ground

Where his feet were.

He took one step forward and my heart was beneath his foot

I was under his control.

*****

In every way he controlled me. And I wanted to break free of his reign.

But I couldn't.

I was somehow trapped in his spell, full of sex and love and hatred for myself.

But the one thing I couldn't let go of

was the person he made me to be.

Without him I felt I had no substance and I was lost in the sea that is him

And the tide welcomed me fully

With open arms.

*****

This is where we stand.

Not upon mountains or cliffs.

We stand not on dry land or sand that sifts.

On each other we lay foot upon chest

We let sadness flow from our veins and hold onto the fears we created for each other.

Time passes and we still stand together like statues in parks.

We are a spectacle for all to see.

*****

Through my sadness I felt you.

I learned everything I needed and I loved you.

And maybe I forgot to love myself.

Or maybe I forgot how to love myself. I'm not sure.

The only thing I know is how to cling to you.

To depend on you.

To love you.

May it be gift or curse

This is the life I live.

The life I will live.

The only life I will ever know.

And through this pain I will lose myself

To win you.

*****

I'm pushing out everything I have. Purging my memories and thoughts. Emptying out my heart and feeding the wolves my soul. I gave up all I could to be his. To be loved by him. To be seen by him. And maybe that wasn't my place. I have always roamed freely till he found me. Or maybe I found him. Maybe I trapped myself. But his love holds me tenderly. At least until he leaves.

But he always comes back.

*****

He gives so much.

And so little

But whatever he gives is always pleasing enough to keep me calm. To keep me from lashing against the fires that surround me as I try to find my way out. He's a wonderful man, don't get me wrong.

But these fires are hot. And grow hotter by the day. And at night they light up our skies and our eyes gloss over with passion and we look up to the sky as the moon is waxing and become two people minus one.

Always minus one.

*****

Like shattered glass, I am broken.

To pieces I will lay on the ground. Sharp with love

And yearning and

The hope that once filled the entirety of me

Has evaporated and now there is nothing

Left but remnants of my soul and the only thing you have

To do now is sweep me off the ground.

*****

I want to be numb to this pain.

I'm tired of feeling so much from so little.

His presence is like a strong flow of light into my dark eyes.

Squinting from pain, I look away from him.

Not once did I want to give up who I was, but look

At me now.

*****

I'm begging you for more.

I cannot stand this solitude. I need you.

But

I have you. So what sense does this make? To keep yearning for a desire that no longer guides your way back to me. This moment. This very second. Every inch of this timeframe.

I spend it thinking of you.

*****

I watch you standing there, so full of the things I long for.

Your touch is unfamiliar to me but I want it. I want to know it.

I want to know you.

But I'm lost in a fantasy world

With you.

*****

He is mute.

To my ears he whispers nothing yet

His silence says everything.

But it means nothing to me, because he does not love me.

He does not care for me.

And my sadness continues

To run its course

Through my veins

I feel remorse

For the love I've given

Was never heard.

*****

My heart is pounding

And the thrill of knowing you is pouring out my mouth.

Feelings I haven't felt in years

Bubble from my throat

And I'm afraid of what I'll find

When it's time to meet you.

Things I'll love

Or things I'll hate

But curiosity is killing me

And I hope it's killing you too.

*****

I've been looking for myself

In others.

And I have found much loneliness

But not much pleasure.

There is some pain

But more than anything I have gained knowledge of life

How people are and how they come to be who they are.

And in all of that I have learned

That life is the toughest lesson

And God is the hardest teacher.

*****

I'm in love with the moon.

It's light holds me

Gives breath to my lungs.

The moon excites me

Makes me feel loved.

But I know I share Her with the rest of the world.

But that's ok.

Because everyone

Has more than one soulmate.

*****

His love feels organic

Because it came from nothing but his flesh and blood.

And no tears to fertilize

But laughs only.

And through the soil of his soul

I felt myself blossom

And leaning towards the light of his heart

I will continue to grow.

*****

I have to thank him

Because without him I would have no words.

There would only be blank pages in my mind.

He forces me to write

Because to him I cannot speak.

My voice is only acceptable

On paper.

*****

His toothy grin made my stomach churn.

With regret I turned away

Because I couldn't bare to be laughed at

Because my voice shook and I knew I sounded foolish.

But I had to speak up

Not only for myself,

But for him as well.

Because if I kept quiet

I was going to commit suicide.

*****

If He's the one, I'm afraid to say

I have no love left.

But I want to give it away

Pour it onto the ground

So he can soak it up.

But the other took it all.

There is nothing left to share.

What's left is just

An empty shell.

*****

You're new to me

But this feeling is familiar.

Same anatomy, different soul.

Yet I'm excited

To experience a new thrill

But the sadness I feel

Is reflected within your eyes.

*****

I don't want to waste your time

But I have a lot to say.

I'm pretty broken

But I'm not all over the place.

My pieces are contained

Within my shell.

So I won't hurt you

When you reach out to touch me.

Just know that I'm fragile.

*****

It was gentle,

The way He touched me.

But my body ached.

And I couldn't sleep that night.

I felt like it was a mistake.

Everything that happened.

Nothing was right about it.

But I won't say it was wrong either.

*****

I'm in love.

I'm not afraid to say it. But I'm afraid of what He will say back.

I'll bite my tongue

Until it's time to be honest.

Until then I'll continue to lie

Beside him

Hoping I'll see mornings with him

Instead of just the night.

*****

The distance between us kills me.

The further he is the harder it is for me

To turn a blind eye.

Because I have fallen for another man

Who holds me closely each night. And though he disappears in the morning

He bridges the gap between us.

*****

Maybe my selfishness caused the troubles we face.

My immaturity and insecurities pushed you away.

I felt weak from love.

It exhausted me, and I could not hide the fact that I was tired.

And you saw this in me.

Passed out on the ground

I watch your feet go past.

*****

He loved me hard.

It was more than anyone could imagine

And more than I could handle.

I was spoiled rotten.

Ruined by his every word and gesture.

And he made sure

That no man could compare.

*****

My love for him was sweet and intoxicating

But I was too emotional to be satisfying.

He didn't care much for my needs or wants

Only for what he could gain.

And what he gained was my wholeness

Everything that made me who I was

And I gave him my mind, body and soul.

And when he kissed my lips

It was like Caramel.

*****

Sometimes I stay awake

Late at night

Waiting for the perfect moment

To write.

I'm anxious to lay out my love for you

To see,

But I'm stuck trying to sleep

Because you only come to me

In my dreams.

*****

Slowly you caressed my skin

And I was left feeling numb.

I wanted to feel more of you

But you held back

Teasing me.

I cried a little. I was lost.

Because I felt that I wasn't whole

Unless you filled me.

*****

Sometimes I wonder if you truly exist.

Because you seem so unreal.

At times, you're heavenly.

Other times, you scorn me.

But either way, I'm in love with

A man

That I barely know.

*****

I'm thinking about you now

Can you feel it?

My thoughts are running wild

In my mind.

I can't control them.

And you couldn't control me.

But I still wanted you to try

Because I'm roaming lonely

Trying to find shelter

In the middle of the night.

*****

I'm getting closer to myself

Through these written accounts.

Whether they be fact or fiction,

My reality or someone else's

They are full of life

And they breathe through voices

Carried out through love.

*****

There's something in the way we connect

I can't quite name it

But I feel it.

It invades my senses,

Like smoke.

It chokes me, blinds me and clouds my mind.

You

Are like smoke to me.

But I don't mind.

*****

I don't think we've met.

But you stopped me in my tracks

And asked where I was heading

And could you join me..

And hesitantly I said

Yes.

Not knowing where I was going myself.

But we walked around aimlessly

Through the night

Howling at the moon.

*****

He had deep scratches in his back

And I was curious

As to who gave them to him

And whether it was out of love or hate.

And I was curious

As to whether I would follow suit

*****

I had him.

The man of my dreams was apart of my reality.

But he didn't stay long.

He left quicker than he came

And I cried

Out his name

Hoping he would come back

Because he didn't get to know me

And I needed to know him

*****

I have a lot of things I want to say to you.

Things I need to let go of

But I can't.

Because you don't care to listen

And once again my voice is falling on deaf ears.

But this time I'm not going to scream.

I won't shout it out to the world

I'll be silent

And still

And wait for the moment where you'll

Truly love me.

*****

This sour taste in my mouth

Will not leave.

Each time I think about you

I feel sick.

The way you hurt me

And embarrassed me.

The way the crowd laughed when I removed the mask I'd been wearing.

All this time I've been hiding

But you brought me out on stage

And for a moment I thought that you would confess your love to me

But instead

You made me out to be a fool.

*****

I lay here next to you

Soaking it all in

The smell of your breath, your warmth, your flesh.

And I'm reminded of the times where

We would sit for hours

Under the moonlight

gathering our voices

Getting lost in each other's words

And learning what it meant to really know someone.

*****

I was having nightmares

Every night. I couldn't sleep.

I was too scared to close my eyes

Because you were there. And I knew in reality

You didn't exist anymore, you had long since disappeared

But at night you came to me

And I couldn't shake the feeling

That maybe you weren't really gone.

*****

You kept getting close to me

And I don't know why I let you in

For so long, I dealt with you.

I tolerated the lies, the women who searched for you every day.

Much to my dismay,

I loved you.

I fell into your spell and I couldn't get out

Like a spider's web,

I was a fly

Trapped.

*****

The light from the Moon never kept me warm, but I always felt peaceful.

I never felt whole, but I always felt pieced together by the brightness.

Being able to stare at her for hours, without risking my eyes

Meant everything to me.

I've never felt more at home

In my own loneliness.

*****

Letting you back in

Is risking my heart

To lots of pain and torture.

But I would rather enjoy the few fleeting moments of happiness I have with you

Than let you go

And never see your face

Or have it light up my skies

Like sunshine.

*****

I tried to stop loving you

I tried to convince myself I didn't care

I tried to tell myself I didn't need you

Or want you

But I was lying.

And in the midst of all my trying

You found someone else

Who danced by your eyes

And she tried to love you

And she tried to convince you that she was the one

Now I'm lying on the ground

Wishing I had tried

A little bit harder.

*****

Why did you tell me that...

Cause I didn't know

That she was the one for you...

Or that..

She shared your heart.

Now my feelings are heavy

Because I have no place to put them.

I thought I could give them to you one day,

But once again I'm left feeling foolish.

My flesh is burning again

I feel like I'm on fire

And there's nothing that can extinguish these flames.

*****

He tempts me...

And there's very little holding me back.

The smell of his power was intoxicating

And I tried to hold onto my sanity

My purity

But

I'm letting thoughts run faster than the speed of light

But all I wish is for him to

Bring me closer to the dark side.

*****

Why don't you love me?

I gave up everything

And I'm left standing here

Lonely and afraid

That I've made a terrible mistake.

But I can't reach you

Because you were already so far away

And you never told me that you had given up.

But your words cut me and your actions stopped me

From caring

So I'm giving up

On you, on love

On us.

*****

I'm sorry for coming to you so late

But I had to see you

I had to get a taste.

My mind was going crazy

Thinking about you

I couldn't help but drive

Thinking about you

To see you

And when I came to the door

In the pouring rain

I whispered your name

As you stared at me in disbelief

And asked why was I here

And before I could utter my reasons

Tempted to pour my heart out on your foyer floor

There she was

In all her glorious skin

Hair sticking to her shoulders

As she peeked over yours

Waiting for me to answer.

*****

I love you

And I wish that I didn't

Because loving you takes too much time

And we have wasted months

Going back and forth

On the idea of us.

And one day you came to me and said

Enough was enough

You've had it with us

But in all honesty

I knew you were tired of me.

Whatever I did to push you away,

I'm sorry.

And to myself,

I'm sorry for you as well

For making you feel this way

For making you love a man

Who doesn't love himself.

*****

It gets harder and harder to wake up everyday

Without you beside me.

The cold sheets remind me

Of a barren wasteland

And I'm stuck

Walking endless miles

Searching for

Your missing soul

That fled from me

In the middle of the night.

*****

I'm feeling frustrated

Because I can't find the words

To say what I mean.

And I'm angry because

You think you have the right

To overtake me

And you are powerless

In all honesty

Against what I am capable of

And the games you seek to play

I'll become victor of.

*****

Grab ahold to my soul

And I'll show you places

You've never seen before

Cross your arms

And close your eyes

Enjoy this mystic ride.

I'm flowing fast

But time feels so slow

Whenever I'm with you

My soul lets go.

*****

Winter, please don't leave me

I love to call your name.

Sometimes the pain

I feel from being with you

Feels good.

You'll never know the feelings you give me

And I'll never be able to express them either.

But every season that rolls around

I pray leaves soon,

Because after fall you'll come to me

Then leave when the flowers bloom.

*****

I want to close my eyes

And have all our troubles melt away.

I want to be able to lay by your side

With not a single care

Or worry or feeling of guilt

Because our life is too short

And our love too fleeting

To waste empty moments

And precious time.

*****

I went to him that night

Because you broke my heart.

He held me in all the right ways

But it didn't feel right.

I missed you

But I didn't want to

Because you threw me aside for her.

And even though you won't admit

I know she exists

Whether she is real or fictional

You left me for another...

I laid in his arms

And cried.

*****

I hear my own voice

Screaming in my head

To let you go, to leave you alone

But I can't.

I can't tell what these feelings are

But they're real and torturing me

Like your eyes do

When you stare at me

And I wonder

What you want to do

When you see me.

*****

Maybe the universe did this to us

Bringing us together

Under unfortunate circumstances.

Then again, it could be nothing.

Either way, things happen

For a reason.

But whatever the reason may be,

We can't ignore it anymore.

We are who they want us to be.

*****

I know you. I knew you. I love you.

Forever, always.

I grew through you, and you through me.

Grateful am I, for your encouraging words

Thoughtful humor

Kind and gentle love.

I'm happy for you.

For the place you're in now, is higher than heaven.

Fly, baby

Fly.

*****

I asked God why did it hurt so much

To be in this place that I'm currently in..I'm drowning, God.

I've been in this water for long enough

But I know how to swim

I just can't.

I have no energy left to exert and God

Oh, God

I'm crying out to you because I feel so helpless

Under his spell

Staring into his deep, dark eyes

I'm drowning in all that is bad

*****

He does something to me

And I can't quite figure it out.

It feels good and it hurts

At the same time

I love to be with him but it brings me great pain.

He's my current world and my dreams

But I'm stuck in a spot

That won't allow me to grow

Because there's no sun besides him

And he's shining on another.

And her petals are softer than mine

Because I'm covered thorns

And I'm painful to touch

But he just can't get enough.

*****

The closer I get to his soul

The warmer I feel

Like there's fire

And I know I'm going to get burned

But I try to remain cool

And calm

Because I don't want the fire to grow

But curiosity

Is my biggest downfall

And I don't know if I'm willing

To throw myself to the Gods just yet.

*****

What I said I wanted

Really wasn't what I meant.

And I'm sorry for what I said,

Now that you're gone.

You're in their arms

and they're wide open for you

As I sit here with my

legs crossed.

*****

I needed you to be who I was searching for.

I needed to give up wanting what I couldn't have.

I needed to learn that life isn't fair

but that love is possible.

*****

It flows freely.

When my mind races,

the thought of our eyes locked

and my legs parted

wrapped around you

holding you tight

and keeping you tighter within me

the feeling of love

rising from the bottom of my soul

and pouring out

from between my legs

Like the Ocean.

*****

I know that

when the time comes

you'll fall in love with me.

Not for what I have

or what I've done.

You'll see me as I am,

Not who I try to be

and

when the time comes

it'll be too late.

*****

In my hands

I hold the power to control my emotions.

But, I sit around and wait

wasting time and energy on you.

This glass is filled half empty

with emotions I can't tolerate

and the smell of sweet

red wine I just can't taste.

Shattered and broken.

The pieces are everywhere

of you, of me, of everything we used to be

Everything we tried to be.

*****

I thought I was past this stage of my life

Dancing with suicide and the thoughts of

Ending the way that I feel.

It's too much. It's too real.

Everything all at once and I just cannot deal.

What brings this pain is not what I want to fall victim to

but,

what am I supposed to do

When all I ever wanted what something I never knew.

*****

I wrote down the frown that was scattered across your face.

You seemed uninterested in what I had to say

but, your gaze met mine

and I felt like I was cracking under the pressure.

I wondered what was going through your mind

Which thoughts were taking over...

*****

He shoved his hands into his pockets, and I instantly felt hopeless.

I knew he had given up on me. My efforts were meaningless and I slid down to the floor, tears filling my eyes.

I wondered if I would ever heal from this

Cause this pain is something I've never experienced before

All in the name of love.

*****

I'm left with two losses-

one is love, the other is life.

I'm not sure when my next chapter will start,

sometimes I question whether this was real

or all in the name of art.

The love I've lost is immeasurable,

from beginning to start.

The life I've lost can't be found

He's floating.

*****

These feelings that rest

underneath my rib cage,

that trickle down my spine

run through my veins

cloud my mind.

The complexities that exist

between you and I

are ones that are mistakenly

beautiful.

*****

You're soft like the light

that comes right before the sun.

Bright but not blinding

No harshness in your lines.

And I'd do anything

to roll over each morning

and catch a glimpse of you

on the other side of my bed.

*****

I could never understand love

and I probably never will.

The pain, the anguish, the

yearning.

It all seems too much to be worth it.

But when you find someone

who, despite all those things,

leaves you wanting more

maybe that's what makes it

Worth it.

*****

You and I

are like art.

We are created with the intention to please

aesthetically.

We mix together to create beautiful colors

and we lie on canvases

blending together

until we become

one.

*****

For those looking for love

In all the wrong places

For those who seek truth

Between lies and anger

For those who are in love

With their own selfish gain

For those who don't know love

Because they don't know pain

For those who love money

And lack the wisdom to realize it

For those who love others

Because they love themselves

For those who love

Simply to love

This was for you.

*

With love,

Mattie.

ABOUT THE AUTHOR

Mattie A. Scott is a storyteller from Atlanta, Georgia.

She has been writing since she was young, using words as an outlet.

She is also a filmmaker who enjoys telling stories through her lens.

She hopes to inspire others through her works.

www.ingramcontent.com/pod-product-compliance
Lightning Source LLC
Chambersburg PA
CBHW060206050426
42446CB00013B/3005